D1709969

21ST
Century
Skills Library

CITIZENS AND THEIR GOVERNMENTS
LAW AND ORDER

Kathleen Manatt

Published in the United States of America by Cherry Lake Publishing
Ann Arbor, MI
www.cherrylakepublishing.com

Photo Credits: Page 7, © Collection of the Supreme Court of the United States;
Page 8, © Collection, The Supreme Court Historical Society, Steve Pettcway;
Page 29, © Photo Courtesy of Eric David Chan

Library of Congress Cataloging-in-Publication Data
Manatt, Kathleen G.
 Law and order / by Kathleen Manatt.
   p. cm. — (Citizens and their governments)
 Includes index.
 ISBN-13: 978-1-60279-064-3
 ISBN-10: 1-60279-064-7
 1. Constitutional law—United States. 2. Courts—United States. 3.
Judges—United States. 4. Law enforcement—United States. 5. United
States. Constitution. I. Title. II. Series.
 KF5130.M36 2008
  342.73—dc22   2007008732

Cherry Lake Publishing would like to acknowledge the work of
The Partnership for 21st Century Skills.
Please visit www.21stcenturyskills.org *for more information.*

TABLE OF CONTENTS

THE U.S. CONSTITUTION

The original U.S. Constitution is kept in the National Archives in Washington, D.C., where citizens and others can view it.

For more than 200 years, our country has been guided by a document called the Constitution. It sets out how leaders will run the country. The United States government is divided into three parts, or branches: the executive, the legislative, and the judicial. Each branch of government has its own responsibilities. The legislative branch is Congress. The executive branch is the president and his or her agents. The judicial branch is the court system.

Why is the government divided up this way? When America's founders wrote the Constitution, they wanted to prevent future leaders from acting unfairly. Dividing the government into branches—a

The Constitution is carefully preserved in the National Archives. In today's world, we can make photocopies of papers or view documents online. Why is it important to preserve original, historical documents such as the Constitution?

system known as "the separation of powers"—provides a system of checks and balances. No one person or group ever becomes too powerful or makes all the decisions. It is a shared responsibility.

Article III

The Constitution is divided into sections called **articles**. Article III describes the judicial branch. This article is shorter than the articles that describe the other two branches. However, the judicial branch is just as powerful. It exists to help people resolve problems with the law or to decide punishment for people who have broken laws. The judicial branch also sometimes decides issues between the other two branches of government.

The Supreme Court was made up of only white men until African-American Thurgood Marshall (top right) was appointed to the court in 1967.

Article III requires that there be one court called the Supreme Court.

It is the most important, or highest, court in the country. This court meets

in Washington, D.C. The court is composed of nine judges, or justices.

Article III also authorizes Congress to set up other, lower courts. These

courts are found all over the country. Article III also ensures the right to

trial by jury in federal courts.

CHAPTER TWO

Courts

*Today's Supreme Court is made up of
blacks and whites, men and women.*

The Supreme Court

The Supreme Court is the head of the judicial branch. The only way to

become a Supreme Court Justice is by appointment. The president is the

only person who has the power to make Supreme Court appointments.

The president appoints someone, and then the Senate must vote to confirm that person. Justices are appointed for life, and many serve on the court for several decades.

Federal Courts

A federal court cannot try to correct a problem on its own. It must have jurisdiction. This means that an appropriate case must be brought before it. Federal courts deal with cases that involve the federal government. They also cover disputes between states or between the federal government and another country.

Federal courts are found in every state. The states are also bundled into groups for higher federal courts. These courts are called district courts and courts of appeal.

One of the basic concepts of American government and the legal system is "the common good." What does this term mean? How does "the common good" affect what you do?

State Courts

Everyday traffic control officers around the world write out parking tickets, and some of the tickets will be disputed in court.

Every state in the United States has its own courts, too. These courts hear cases for just their state. They deal with everything from parking tickets to murder cases. They settle disputes about who owns land. They control cases about robbery and trespassing. They administer property distribution after somebody dies. They oversee marriages and divorces.

Just like federal courts, state courts have several levels. At the top is a state supreme court. However, below that level of court there are many variations. For example, Texas has five levels of state courts, but Illinois has only three. It is up to the state to decide, and the decisions are laid out in the state constitution. No matter how many levels of courts, each state may need hundreds or even thousands of judges to run its court system.

Why do California and Texas need many more judges than North Dakota and Vermont? *Hint*: Think about population.

CHAPTER THREE

JUDGES AND JURIES

Judges

Judges in America are black, white, Asian, Hispanic, male, female, young, and old.

Being a judge is a big deal! Judges are important people and are greatly respected. In the United States, a judge is addressed as "Your Honor" or "Judge" when court is in session. These titles show the respect others have for the role of judges. Often, judges are addressed as "Your Honor" or "Judge" when away from court, too.

Some judges are appointed to their positions.

The justices of the Supreme Court are some of them.

Other federal judges are appointed, too.

Other judges are often elected. Like other elected

officials, these judges have set terms, such as two or

four years. Then they must run for office again. Many

state court judges are elected. However, different

states have different laws about how their judges will

be chosen.

Members of the military are addressed by their rank, such as captain, sergeant, or general. What are some other jobs where a person is often addressed by title or rank?
Hint: Think about the last time you had to get a shot.

Judges issue search warrants for specific places, such as a home, business, or car, and law officers can only look there.

Judges perform many tasks. For example, they listen to police officers tell why the officers need a **search warrant**. These documents give police officers permission to search a specific place, such as a car or office, for evidence. If the judge agrees that the officers have a good reason to search a place, the judge will sign the search warrant. If the police officers do not have a search warrant, anything they find might not be legally used in a trial.

During a trial, the judge runs things. The judge decides what time of day the trial will start and when everybody will go to lunch. The judge maintains order in the courtroom, with help from the bailiff. Judges are very careful to follow the law when doing their jobs. Otherwise, one of the two sides in the trial may ask for a new trial after this one is over!

Think of a time when you had to follow rules instead of doing what you felt like doing. What was the result?

Most judges in the United States were lawyers before they became judges. Many wear black robes as a symbol of their roles.

The judge decides issues when the lawyers

disagree. For example, the lawyers may disagree

about who can testify. The judge will listen to

lawyers from both sides talk, and then the judge

will decide.

In a criminal trial, the judge makes sure

that the defendant gets a fair and speedy trial.

Such a trial is promised in the U.S. Constitution.

Sometimes, judges also decide on punishment

when a defendant is found to be guilty.

One of the nicest duties that judges have is the right to marry people! Usually such marriages take place in the judge's chambers or some place other than a church, mosque, or synagogue. Why do you need to check laws and regulations when you plan to get married?

*Most Americans are notified by mail that
they have been selected for jury duty.*

The Jury

A **jury** is a group of citizens chosen to decide the truth in a legal

case. Many juries have 12 people, but some juries have fewer. The

jury members attend court every day. They listen carefully to all the

evidence that is presented. They also listen carefully to anything the judge tells them. Then the jury meets alone and decides the verdict. Sometimes, the jury members can't decide. Then the whole court case must begin again.

Any adult citizen can be asked to be on a jury. This includes doctors, ministers, governors, teachers, and even judges! Usually if a person is not picked for a specific jury in a day or week, that person is excused from jury duty for at least a year.

People on jury duty must miss work. They may lose pay, too. However, the American court system cannot function without individual citizens doing their duty.

Learning & Innovation Skills

It is our duty as Americans to serve on juries when asked to do so. Do you think it would be fair to take away the right to a jury trial from someone who "got out of" jury duty? Why or why not?

In the American legal system, there are two sides in every court case.

Sometimes the case is just between two people. Other times, the case is

between the government and a person. In both types of cases, lawyers

represent each side. In big, complicated cases, there may be whole teams of

lawyers for each side. However, there is always just one jury.

In most trials the lawyers and their clients sit at tables facing the judge

CHAPTER FOUR

TRIALS

Although courtrooms might be organized differently, all participants face the judge.

There are two kinds of trials. A civil trial is one kind. One person or

group says that another has done something wrong to them. They take the

issue to court to let a judge, and sometimes a jury, decide. A **criminal trial** is the other kind. It decides on charges made by the government that a person—or persons—has committed a crime. Thousands of both kinds of trials take place every year.

Lawyers

These thousands of trials require thousands and thousands of lawyers. In fact, there are hundreds of thousands of lawyers in the United States. The American Bar Association has more than 400,000 members.

Many lawyers specialize in certain kinds of court cases. For example, some lawyers handle only divorce cases. Some lawyers work for the government and prosecute criminals. Other lawyers only defend people who have been accused of crimes.

Whatever kind of trial it is, the lawyers do most of the talking. They speak to the jury at the beginning of the case to tell their side of the issue. They question witnesses. They ask the judge to decide other issues that come up. The lawyers also speak to the jury at the end of the trial. At this time, the lawyers review the facts of the case and try to make the jury decide in their favor.

21st Century Content

Being a lawyer requires at least three years of school beyond college. Then the lawyer must take a statewide test. If the lawyer passes the test, then he or she can work in that state. The focus of legal training is understanding American law and applying it to specific situations. A student interested in a legal career can start with a solid civic literacy.

CHAPTER FIVE

Law Enforcement

Like others who testify during a trial, law enforcement officers must also swear to be truthful in what they say.

Police officers and other law enforcement people play a big role in criminal cases. If a crime is committed, they look for evidence and other clues. Then they study the evidence and clues to help them figure out who might have committed the crime. Once they think they know who the criminal is, they search for and arrest that person. Then during the trial, law enforcement people may be asked to testify about events, evidence, and clues.

Federal Law Enforcement

Several groups in the federal government are made up of law enforcement people. One major group is the Federal Bureau of Investigation,

21st Century Content

There are FBI offices in many American cities, including New York, Los Angeles, El Paso, Chicago, Tampa, Indianapolis, San Diego, and Mobile. Why might the number of people assigned to the Chicago, Illinois, office be more than that assigned to the office in Mobile, Alabama? *Hint*: Think about population.

or FBI. Its agents search for kidnappers, bank robbers, and terrorists, among others. Overall, the FBI is responsible for investigating more than 200 types of crimes. They also investigate crimes on Native American reservations. The FBI has offices in almost every state and in many big cities, too.

Other federal law enforcement groups include the Secret Service and the Postal Service Inspectors. The Secret Service protects the president, vice president, their families, and visiting heads of state. Agents also investigate cases of counterfeit, or fake, money and cases involving fake credit cards.

Postal Service Inspectors investigate crimes that use the mail, telephone, or sometimes even the Internet. For example, they investigate "get rich quick schemes" that convince people to send money through the mail for investments that don't exist.

Local Law Enforcement

Just as the federal government has special groups that enforce the law and investigate crimes, so do states, cities, and counties. For sure, your town or city has police officers. Some of these people may just check to see if cars are parked legally. Other officers may investigate murders and robberies. No matter

Learning & Innovation Skills

Just like hospitals, police stations never close. Why is that? *Hint*: Think about only being sick between 9 A.M. and 5 P.M.

what the officers do, they may be called upon to come to court to testify about matters they have worked on.

The Big Picture

Maintaining law and order in the United States—or any nation—is a big, complex job. It requires people with many different skills and types of education. Law enforcement people must investigate crimes and arrest suspects. Lawyers, judges, and juries of citizens must all participate in trials. Everyone must do his or her best so that all citizens trust the American system of law and order. No matter what part you play in the system, success is up to you!

A trial can last from less than one day to several months or more.

GLOSSARY

appointment (uh-POINT-muhnt) act of selecting or designating someone for an office or position

articles (AHR-ti-kuhls) name given to major sections of the U.S. Constitution

bailiff (BEY-lif) person in courtroom responsible for maintaining order

civil trial (SIV-uhl TRAHY-uhl) trial between two parties

criminal trial (KRIM-uh-nl TRAHY-uhl) trial in which the government has brought charges

defendant (di-FEN-dant) person or group charged with a crime in a criminal trial

executive (ig-ZEK-yuh-tiv) branch of the federal government made up of the president and his or her agents

judicial (joo-DISH-uhl) branch of the federal government made up of the court system

jurisdiction (joor-is-DIK-shuhn) right and power to interpret and apply the law

jury (JOOR-ee) citizens chosen to hear evidence in a trial and decide the outcome

justices (JUHS-tis-ez) name for judges of the U.S. Supreme Court

legislative (LEJ-is-ley-tiv) branch of the federal government made up of Congress

prosecute (PROS-i-kyoot) to begin and conduct legal proceedings

search warrant (surch WAWR-uhnt) document giving legal authority for a search

Supreme Court (suh-PREEM kohrt) highest court in the United States

testify (TES-tuh-fahy) to speak in court under oath

verdict (VUR-dikt) formal decision or finding made by a jury at the end of a trial

FOR MORE INFORMATION

Books

De Capua, Sarah. *Serving on a Jury.*
New York: Children's Press, 2002.

Egan, Tim. *The Trial of Cardigan Jones.*
Boston: Houghton Mifflin, 2004.

Jacobs, Thomas A. *Teens Take It to Court: Young People Who
Challenged the Law—and Changed Your Life.*
Minneapolis: Free Spirit Publishing, 2006.

January, Brendan. *The Supreme Court.* New York: Scholastic, 2004.

McElroy, Lisa Tucker. *Meet My Grandmother: She's a Supreme
Court Justice.* Brookfield, CT: Milbrook Press, Inc., 1999.

Quiri, Patricia Ryan. *The Supreme Court.*
New York: Children's Press, 1998.

Other Media

Thurgood Marshall: Justice for All. DVD. A&E Home Video, 2005.

INDEX

ABOUT THE AUTHOR

Kathleen Manatt is a long-time writer, editor, and publisher of books for children. Many of her books have been about faraway places, which she likes to visit. She grew up in Illinois, Iowa, New Jersey, and California, and lived in Chicago for many years as an adult. She has climbed pyramids in Mexico, ridden elephants in Thailand, and toured the fjords of Norway. She has also visited Moscow, Lisbon, Paris, Geneva, London, Madrid, Edinburgh, and Barcelona. She now lives in Austin, Texas.

ML

12/09